Garden Edges & Retaining Walls

FRANK GARDNER

MINI · WORKBOOK · SERIES

MURDOCH
B O O K S

CONTENTS

GARDEN EDGES AND RAISED BEDS

RETAINING WALLS

Timber edging (top), dry-stone retaining wall (far left) and rendered masonry retaining wall (left)

This raised bed provides ideal conditions for plants and breaks up a large expanse of wall. Both wall and bed have been given a rendered finish.

Garden edges and raised beds

Garden edges, whether flat or raised, are primarily used to contain garden beds, but they are also an integral part of the garden landscape and should be planned accordingly.

PLANNING GARDEN EDGES

Begin by drawing a detailed plan of your house and land. Each line that you draw will require some form of edge. It may be a flat edge (often a mowing strip), a raised kerb to retain garden or lawn or to control the flow of water, or a raised garden bed.

Next, you need to decide on the edging material. Consider the style of your home, the degree of formality required, the amount of money you have to spend and how readily the material is available. As well as the materials discussed below there are less permanent materials, such as plants or the wire borders so popular with Victorian and Edwardian gardeners (and now available again from most garden suppliers).

BRICKS, PAVING AND TILES

Dry-pressed house bricks, which have a 'frog' (a depression) on one side, are better for edges than extruded bricks, which have holes running right through the brick.

Raised brick edges can sit directly on the soil, but to prevent sideways movement they are best contained on one side by a solid surface and on the other by a buttress of concrete.

Clay paving stones are used for flat edges such as mowing strips and are laid on the flat, while terracotta tiles are used for raised edges and can be positioned in straight, curved or geometric lines. Like bricks, they are best supported by a solid surface and concrete buttress.

STONE

Stone makes an excellent hard-wearing edging for the garden. It can be cut into regular shapes and the blocks butted closely together, or mortared as for brickwork. If the blocks are laid flush with the ground, a mowing strip will not be necessary. Undressed stone can be laid with or without mortared joints.

CONCRETE

Concrete can be used to make edgings of any shape or height. It has traditionally been neutral in colour, but the use of oxides to colour concrete is increasingly popular. Concrete strips can also be stamped or stencilled in a variety of patterns.

Precast concrete strips are available from garden supply centres. They are most suitable for straight edging where lengths can be butted together. Other concrete products, such as cobblestones and paving stones, are laid in the same way as bricks.

TIMBER

The simplest form of timber edging consists of lengths of timber (treated pine or durable hardwood) laid horizontally on edge and held in place by timber or metal pegs. When laid horizontally, such timbers are suitable only for straight edging. For curved edges, install them vertically, stacked closely side by side. They can be cut off in a level line or the height can be staggered to create a one-up, one-down effect.

Old (recycled) and new railway sleepers make ideal edges. They are heavy to move but are strong and fairly durable. Their own weight is usually enough to hold them in place, whether bedded at ground level or raised to create an edge.

RAISED GARDEN BEDS

Raised beds are used to create different levels within the garden, either for aesthetic reasons or to give greater control over growing conditions. Unless you have free-draining, sandy soil you will have to make provision for drainage, usually by making weep holes just above ground level every 600 mm or so. It is also a good idea to place a 100 mm deep bed of crushed rock, tile or broken brick in the base of the bed before filling it with soil.

Sawtooth brick edging

House bricks make an easy-to-lay raised edging that will not move when held in place by a solid surface and concrete buttress. The same method is used for sawtooth or on-end patterns.

METHOD

1 If necessary, construct a concrete mowing strip along the front of the edging position (see pages 14–17).

2 Excavate a trench 200 mm wide and 100 mm below the top of the concrete or paved surface. Use a

TOOLS AND MATERIALS

- Basic tools (see page 13)
- Sliding bevel or 45-degree set square
- Dry-pressed house bricks
- Cement, sharp sand and 10 mm aggregate (gravel)

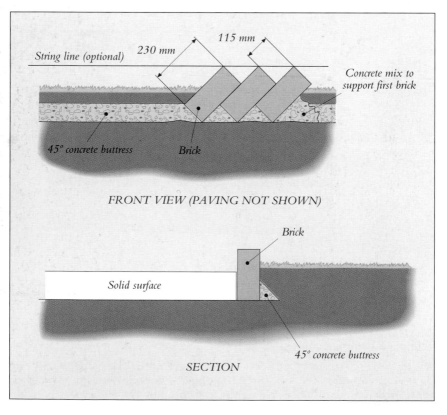

FRONT VIEW (PAVING NOT SHOWN)

SECTION

To create this attractive sawtooth edging, bricks were placed at an angle of 45 degrees and supported with mortar packing. A concrete buttress at the back holds them firmly against the paving.

spirit level to check if the ground is level; otherwise the edge will have to follow the contour of the ground.

3 Make a stiff 1:6 mix of concrete or mortar using sharp sand. Begin laying the bricks from one end of the edging, as they 'piggy-back' on one another. Using a sliding bevel set at 45 degrees, position the first brick at an angle of 45 degrees. Pack mortar beneath this brick to hold it in place.

4 Continue laying the bricks, placing them either by measuring or by using a string line. The string line method is suitable only for straight edges.

• To lay by measuring, calculate half the length of a brick (most are 215 mm long so that half is usually 107 mm). Using a measuring tape, position each brick 107 mm down the back of the previous brick until the edge is completed.

• Alternatively, set a taut, level string line from the top of the first brick along the line of the proposed edge. Position each subsequent brick down the back of the previous brick, in line and level with the string line.

THE 3-4-5 METHOD

The 3-4-5 method is a simple way to ensure you have made a right-angled corner. From the corner point measure down one side 300 mm and down the other 400 mm (or you can use any multiples of these numbers, for example, 3 m and 4 m or 600 mm and 800 mm). The hypotenuse (diagonal) should equal 500 mm (or the appropriate multiple) if you have made a right-angle triangle.

5 To hold the bricks firmly in place, lay a concrete buttress (see page 27 for mixing concrete) against the inside edge, also pushing concrete beneath the gap under each brick to prevent the bricks sinking. Using a steel or wooden float, batter the concrete at an angle of about 45 degrees to form a buttress.

6 Allow time for the concrete to dry before filling in behind the bricks with soil.

3 Using a sliding bevel set at an angle of 45 degrees, position the first brick for the edging.

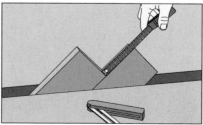

4 Using the measuring tape, position each subsequent brick 107 mm down the back of the previous brick.

A WATER LEVEL

A water level is useful when you have to find the same level at a number of points over uneven ground. It is accurate to 1–2 mm. Two people are needed to use it.

1 Purchase 10 m of 10 mm (internal measurement) diameter clear plastic tubing and two stoppers to fit tightly into the ends of the tubing as plugs. Fill the tubing with water, releasing all air bubbles, and add drops of food colouring so the water is easier to see. Leave 400 mm empty either end so the water can fluctuate. Insert the plugs in either end.

2 Remove the plugs but place a thumb over each end of the tubing to prevent loss of water. Position one end of the tubing at the established mark and the other end where a new level mark is needed.

3 Remove your thumbs to allow the water to move. When it has settled, adjust the water level at the established mark until the base of the meniscus in the tubing is in line with the mark.

4 At the other end, the base of the meniscus indicates the level mark. Keeping one end at the original mark, you can move the other end around to any number of points.

5 When you have finished, replace the stoppers in both ends.

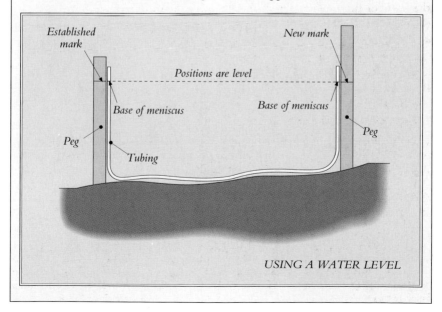

USING A WATER LEVEL

Natural stone was used to edge this garden bed while retaining the informal character of the garden. As it was built against existing paving, a mowing strip to hold the stones in place was not necessary.

Stone edging

Stone makes a hard-wearing edging for the garden, and one that looks entirely natural. In this project undressed stone was set into a bed of mortar to make a raised edge.

LAYING STONE EDGES

Stone is usually available from garden supply centres. It is sold by the square metre: the amount you will need can be worked out for you by the supplier, based on the length of your edging. Flat-faced, chunky stones are most suitable for close-butted, unmortared joints.

When you are using irregularly shaped stones, you should construct a mower strip if the edge is against lawn. All stone edges should be fixed in place by bedding the stones into a 20–50 mm footing of concrete.

Free-flowing curves can be more easily laid using irregularly shaped stone than dressed blocks.

PREPARATION

1 If you are not working against an existing surface, establish the line by setting a string line. For curved edges lay out a rope or garden hose, or you can sprinkle flour or lime to mark the curve.

2 Excavate approximately 100 mm below ground level so that all grass and vegetation are removed. The width of the excavation should be approximately 300 mm but will vary according to the size of the stone. If

> ### TOOLS AND MATERIALS
> - Basic tools (see page 13)
> - Natural (undressed) stone
> - Cement
> - Sand
> - 10 mm aggregate (gravel)

you need to add a mower strip, increase the footing width by 100 mm and make a 100 mm vertical cut at the front of the excavation.

LAYING THE STONE

3 Lay out the stone approximately 500 mm in front of the excavated edge. This will give you a rough idea of how the edging will look. Reposition individual pieces of stone, turning them over or around or swapping them with other pieces until you are satisfied with how they will butt together. If you want the top edge of the stones to be level, adjust the depth of the trench to suit each stone (see the diagram on page 13). If the top of the edging is to be irregular, however, the stones can be placed on a flat bed.

4 Prepare the ground for concrete by wetting it to prevent the concrete

bed drying and hardening too quickly. It is advisable to mix your own concrete so that small sections can be laid at a time. This avoids the problem of a whole load of commercially delivered concrete going hard before all the stone is laid. See page 27 for instructions on mixing concrete.

5 Spread a bed of 50 mm thick concrete approximately 1 m long. Position each stone in turn, using the string line as a guide for an even top edge. Give each stone two or three twists to bed it firmly in place. Make sure each stone is hard up against the edge and also closely butted against the last stone.

6 Fill any gaps with small pieces of stone. Cut them to fit with a club hammer and bolster and tap them in place. Use concrete at the back of each joint to prevent soil washing out through the joints.

TO FINISH

7 Fill any narrow gaps between the stones and the hard edge with a sand

---

USING MORTARED JOINTS

To mortar the joints between the stones, follow the steps on pages 11–12 but space the stones approximately 50 mm apart.

Mix a fairly stiff mortar mix of four parts sand and one part cement. Coloured oxides can be added to the mortar so the joints blend naturally with the rock.

Wearing protective gloves, roll the mix in your hands to make large sausage shapes of mortar. Place each 'sausage' in a joint and use a small trowel to work the mortar in and round the joint.

Use a small paintbrush to finish the surface of the joints and then sponge the face of the stone until it is clean.

---

and cement grout, or sand. Allow the concrete to dry before filling in behind the edging with garden soil.

8 If necessary, add a mower strip at the front of the stone edging (see pages 14–17).

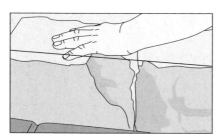

5 Position each stone in turn, using the string line as a guide and bedding each firmly in place.

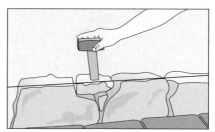

6 Fill any gaps by tapping small pieces of stone, which have been cut to fit, into place.

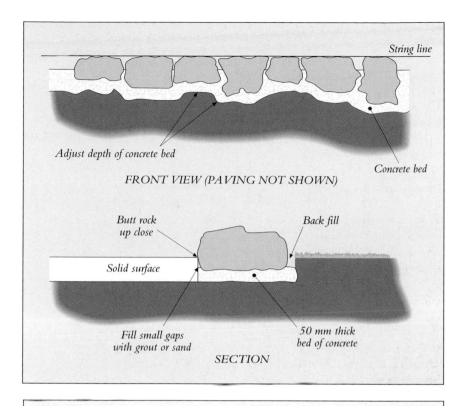

String line

Adjust depth of concrete bed

Concrete bed

FRONT VIEW (PAVING NOT SHOWN)

Butt rock up close

Back fill

Solid surface

Fill small gaps with grout or sand

50 mm thick bed of concrete

SECTION

BASIC TOOLS

There are a number of basic tools required for any construction project in the garden, whether it is a simple edging or a retaining wall. If you have the tools on the following list, you can be sure you will have all the tools you need for a satisfactory job.

- Measuring tape
- Spirit level
- String line
- Shovel
- Spade

- Rake
- Mattock
- Claw hammer
- Club hammer
- Bolster
- Handsaw
- Steel float
- Wooden float
- Permanent black marking pen
- Broom
- Hose
- Wheelbarrow

Concrete mowing strip

Concrete is a very versatile edging material and is particularly useful for a curved or irregular edge. It can be coloured or treated to match most natural products used in the garden.

PREPARATION

1 Determine the position of the mowing strip.

- To lay out a straight strip, use a string line between two pegs.
- For a curved strip, sprinkle flour or lime on the ground or lay a length of rope or the garden hose where you want it to be. Avoid sharp bends and corners, as it is difficult to flex the timber formwork around them and they are difficult to edge neatly. If sharp bends are necessary and the timber fails to flex sufficiently, use vinyl or strong plastic as formwork.
- To make a neat semicircular shape, drive a short peg into the centre of the area (see the diagram on page 16). Hammer a 25 x 2 mm clout nail into the top of the peg, leaving 10 mm of nail exposed. Attach a string line to the top of the nail, stretch it taut, loop a long stick at the end of it and scribe a semicircle.

2 Hammer small pegs along the line every 800 or 1000 mm. Excavate the ground along the line to a depth of 100 mm and a width of 200 mm.

3 Using pine offcuts clear of knots, set up the outside formwork. (Having a helper makes this job

TOOLS AND MATERIALS
• Basic tools (see page 13)
• 75 mm edging tool
• Jointing tool
• Timber pegs
• 100 x 10 mm pine offcuts (splits)
• 25 x 2 mm flat-headed clout nails
• Timber blocks or bricks
• Cement
• Fine-grained sand such as beach sand
• 10 mm aggregate (gravel)

easier, as it is difficult to flex and hold the timber to the correct curve, and also peg and nail at the same time.) To hold the formwork in place, use sufficient timber pegs to prevent it bulging out of shape when it is filled with concrete. One peg per metre should suffice. Nail through the formwork and then into the peg, using 25 x 2 mm clout nails.

4 Once the outside formwork is in place, repeat the procedure for the inside formwork. As you work, insert timber blocks or bricks to keep the sides of the formwork the correct distance apart and parallel. A strip 100 mm wide is usually suitable, but

A concrete edging for this semicircular garden bed was easily built using basic concreting equipment. Concrete is just as suitable for constructing edges that are straight or irregularly curved.

it can be wider or narrower as you prefer. Timber blocks can be partially fixed with nails if they won't hold in position. Use a spirit level to make sure the tops of the formwork strips are level. The tops of the formwork should also be level with the ground if the strip is to be a functional mower strip.

LAYING THE CONCRETE

5 Mix the concrete (see the box on page 27). Shovel it into the formwork, removing one spacer at a

4 Using spacing blocks and a spirit level to make sure the tops are level, erect the inner side of the formwork.

5 Using a float, pack the concrete so that the surface is level with the top of the formwork.

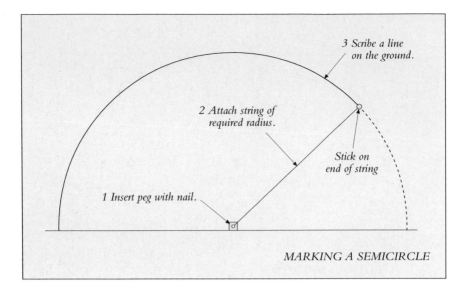

3 Scribe a line on the ground.

2 Attach string of required radius.

Stick on end of string

1 Insert peg with nail.

MARKING A SEMICIRCLE

time as the formwork is filled. Tap the sides of the formwork with a hammer or mallet to settle the concrete and remove air pockets. Using a float, pack and level the surface to the top of the formwork.

6 Use the edging tool to edge the strip on both sides and to push the gravel down into the concrete so that you have a smooth, neat finish when the concrete is dry.

7 Control joints allow the concrete to crack without ruining the appearance of the strip. To make control joints, mark every 1500 mm along the formwork. Hold the jointing tool against a straight edge and cut a joint onto the surface of the concrete. Move the tool lightly back and forth to obtain a neat finish. For the best effect, the control joints should be completely straight, and they should be evenly spaced.

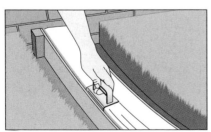

6 Use an edging tool to edge the strip on both sides and push the gravel down for a smooth finish.

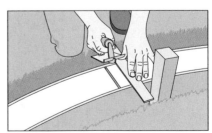

7 Hold the tool against a straight edge and cut a control joint every 1500 mm to hide future cracking.

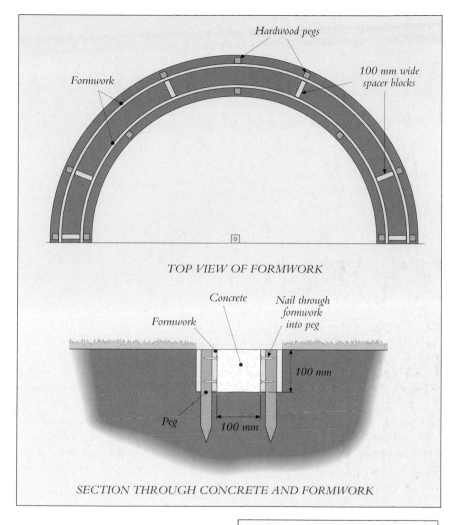

Hardwood pegs

Formwork

100 mm wide
spacer blocks

TOP VIEW OF FORMWORK

Concrete

Nail through
formwork
into peg

Formwork

100 mm

Peg

100 mm

SECTION THROUGH CONCRETE AND FORMWORK

8 To finish, allow the strip to dry until only the surface is workable. For a grainy finish move a wooden float over it in a circular motion. A steel float provides a smooth finish.

9 Refinish the joints and edging. Allow the concrete to dry for 2–3 days before removing the formwork.

COLOURING CONCRETE

Concrete can be coloured by:
• adding pigment while mixing the concrete;
• shaking dry pigment over the surface during the final floating;
• using paving paint on concrete that has already dried.

Treated pine rails make a neat garden edging. They can also be used to make a mowing strip if they are set into the ground beside lawn.

Timber edging

Timber is a quick way of providing an edging and it is particularly useful for retaining loose landscaping materials such as woodchip, bark or pebbles.

SELECTING TIMBER

Timber used for garden edging is in constant contact with the ground and must be able to withstand damp and attack by insects. Softwoods that have been treated to withstand attack by insects, fungi and damp, and durable hardwoods are both suitable for garden edges but the treated softwoods are easier to work.

Preservative-treated softwoods have been treated with compounds of copper, chromium and arsenic (CCA) and they are given a rating of between low and high according to their hazard level (low is the least durable and, therefore, the least hazardous). This rating is branded on the timber. Always wear gloves when handling this material and a dust mask when sawing it. Do not burn any offcuts, as the smoke and ash are also toxic.

When using treated timber as garden edging, select timber with at least a medium-high rating. If you cut the timber, the new surfaces will have to be resealed with preservative to ensure resistance to attack.

The lengths of timber available from timber merchants usually start at 1.8 m, with lengths increasing by increments of 0.3 m. Timber can be ordered as rough-sawn or planed all round (PAR). Timber that is planed all round has had all four surfaces machine planed to a smooth finish. This reduces the finished size of the timber but it makes it easier to paint or stain it.

METHOD

1 Determine the layout of the edging by setting string lines in the desired location, and at the desired finished height if possible. Excavate along this line to a width of 100 mm and a depth of 120 mm below the string line, and remove all vegetable matter from the area.

TOOLS AND MATERIALS

- Basic tools (see page 13)
- Circular saw or handsaw
- 10 mm crushed rock (gravel)
- 70 x 35 mm timber rails (preservative-treated pine or hardwood)
- 70 x 35 mm timber pegs (preservative-treated pine or hardwood)
- 50 x 2.8 mm twisted flat-head galvanised nails
- 70 x 3.5 mm twisted flat-head galvanised nails

2 Lay a bed of 10 mm diameter gravel about 50 mm deep in the base of the trench. Spread the gravel evenly and make it as level as possible to provide a good drainage base for the timber, thus extending its life.

3 Position the rails on edge below the set string lines or to match the existing ground level.

4 Position a timber peg against the inner face of the rail every 1200 mm. Using a club hammer, drive in the timber pegs until they are firmly embedded. The top of the peg

3 Position the rails on edge below the set string lines or so that they match the existing ground level.

4 Drive in the pegs until they are firmly embedded and the tops are 25–30 mm below the top of the rail.

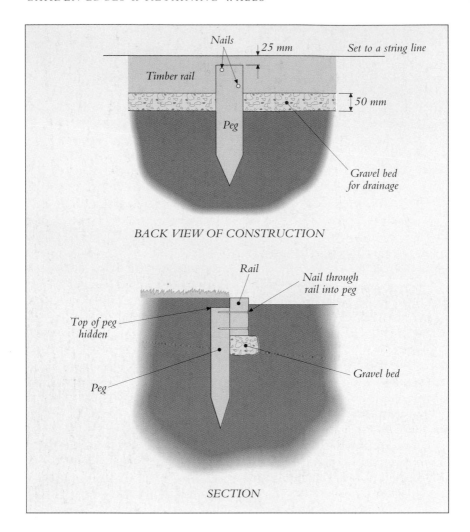

Nails

25 mm   Set to a string line

Timber rail

50 mm

Peg

Gravel bed
for drainage

BACK VIEW OF CONSTRUCTION

Rail

Nail through
rail into peg

Top of peg
hidden

Peg

Gravel bed

SECTION

should be approximately 25–30 mm below the top of the rail so that the peg can be covered with lawn, soil or bark and thus hidden.

5 Fix the rails in place by nailing through the rail and into the peg with 50 x 2.8 mm twisted flat-head galvanised nails. Use at least two nails

for each peg and place them diagonally for added strength.

6 If the timber rails have to be joined, you can use a butt, lap or scarf joint (see the diagram on page 21), but the scarf joint is less obvious and provides greater strength. Position a peg at the joint and nail

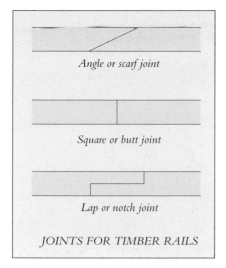

Angle or scarf joint

Square or butt joint

Lap or notch joint

JOINTS FOR TIMBER RAILS

through the joint into the peg, using 70 x 3.5 mm twisted flat-head galvanised nails. To construct a 90-degree corner, use a mitre box or mitre saw to make 45 degree cuts in the rails.

7 If you are using treated pine, reseal any cut surfaces to ensure resistance to decay. Dispose of offcuts properly by burying them (usually at the tip). If desired, finish the rails with exterior surface paint.

5 Nail through the rail and into the peg with two offset 50 x 2.8 mm twisted flat-head galvanised nails.

MAKING A SCARF JOINT

1 Measure 50 mm back from the edge of the rail, or the required distance (the diagonal cut can be longer than the width—it does not have to be a 45-degree cut).

2 Using a square, draw a line across the rail at this point.

3 Draw a diagonal line from the squared line back to the corner of the rail.

4 Cut along the diagonal using a power saw or handsaw.

5 Place the second rail over the cut, mark it to match the first rail, and cut it.

6 Fit the two rails together and nail across the joint, using at least two nails.

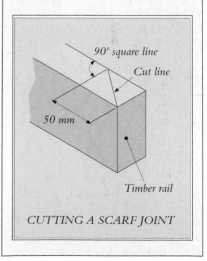

90° square line

Cut line

50 mm

Timber rail

CUTTING A SCARF JOINT

Brick raised bed

Three courses of brickwork are used for this raised bed, with the curved wall and top course of the straight walls laid header style. The walls rest on a solid concrete footing.

MATERIALS

- 100 x 50 mm timber for straight formwork
- 100 x 10 mm split pine timber for curved formwork
- Timber pegs (up to 1 m long)
- 25 x 2 mm galvanised clout nails
- 65 x 3 mm lost-head nails
- Three-bar steel reinforcement, tie wire and bar men
- Cement
- Sand
- Coarse aggregate (gravel)
- Lime or fireclay
- Plasticiser
- Bricks

TOOLS

- Basic tools (see page 13)
- Builders' square
- Water level
- Steel mesh cutters or angle grinder
- Concrete mixer (if available)
- Mortar board
- Brick saw or circular saw with masonry blade
- Line pins and corner blocks for holding string line (optional)
- Bricklaying trowel
- Joint raker
- Brush
- Sponge
- Bucket

PREPARING THE FOOTING

1 Determine the position and shape of the garden bed. Consider the size of your bricks and calculate so that you can use as many whole bricks as possible to reduce the number of bricks you need to cut.

2 Peg out the area, setting string lines for the straight sides, and sprinkling flour or lime or using a rope or garden hose for the front curve. Make the curve as gradual as possible, to keep the need to cut bricks to a minimum. Ensure that the back corner is square by using either a builders' square or the 3-4-5 method (see the box on page 8).

3 Excavate the area to a depth of 100 mm or as required (see the box on page 33). Remove all vegetation.

4 Position 1 m long pegs in each corner and hammer them into the ground until they are firm. On one peg mark 500 mm above ground level. Use a water level to transfer

This brick bed requires only basic bricklaying skills to construct and yet makes a very attractive addition to the garden. The size of the concrete footing is adjusted to suit the size of the plants the bed will contain.

this accurately to the other corner pegs (see the box on page 9). To obtain the finished height of the concrete footing, which is the top of the formwork, measure down 500 mm from the water level marks.

5 Attach string lines on the two straight sides at this height and set the formwork. Hold the straight timber in place with pegs every 1200 mm. The space between the two sides of the formwork should be 300 mm. To form up the curved front edge, use split pine lengths which have sufficient flexibility to bend. Use a spirit level to ensure that the formwork is level and 500 mm below the water level marks. Time spent positioning the formwork accurately to create a level footing will make the bricklaying easier.

6 For a 100 mm deep footing, position one layer of three-bar

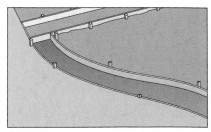

5 To form up the curved front edge, use split pine lengths which have sufficient flexibility to bend.

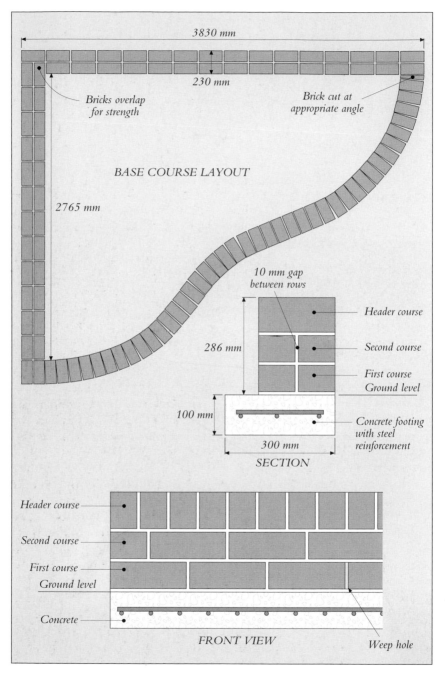

3830 mm

230 mm

*Bricks overlap
for strength*

*Brick cut at
appropriate angle*

BASE COURSE LAYOUT

2765 mm

*10 mm gap
between rows*

286 mm

Header course

Second course

First course
Ground level

100 mm

*Concrete footing
with steel
reinforcement*

300 mm

SECTION

Header course

Second course

First course
Ground level

Concrete

FRONT VIEW

Weep hole

reinforcing steel within the formwork on bar men and tie it together at the corners. To bend the straight mesh around the front curve, cut it in several places, kink it around the curve and tie it back together with tie wire.

7 Mix the concrete (see page 27). Fill the footing with concrete. Use a short piece of timber to screed off the concrete with a sawing motion and then finish the surface with a wooden float. Use a straight length of timber with a spirit level on top to check the surface is level. Allow the concrete to set for 2–3 days. Remove the formwork.

LAYING THE BRICKS

8 Use a builders' square to check that the back corner is at 90 degrees. Mark starting points on the footing to ensure full bricks will fit.

9 Prepare a mortar mix of five parts sand, one part cement and half a part of lime or fireclay (5:1:½). A plasticiser can also be added to make the mix more workable. Mix the dry

7 Fill the footing with concrete and use a piece of timber to screed off the concrete with a sawing motion.

materials together thoroughly in a wheelbarrow and then add enough water to make a pliable mix with the consistency of toothpaste. Mortar is useful for only about one and a half hours, so don't mix too much at a time. If you are using a cement mixer, double the mix to 10:2:1 and use one-third of a cup of plasticiser for two shovels of cement.

10 Transfer the mortar to a mortar board. To keep it soft and pliable, work it back and forth across the board with a trowel. Construct the straight walls first. Begin at the back corner, building it to the height of two courses and overlapping the bricks for strength. Leave a gap of precisely 10 mm between the rows so that when the header course is placed across the double row of brickwork, the sides will be vertical.

11 Set taut string lines for both sides of each wall. Build the ends of the walls to two courses in the same way.

12 Set the string lines for the base course. Spread a double line of mortar onto the footing and fill in the first double row of brickwork. As you pick up each brick, butter (apply mortar to) one end and position it on the bed of mortar, butting up to the last brick laid. Use the trowel to tap the brick into position so that the joints are maintained at a consistent 8–10 mm spacing. Use a spirit level to double check that the course is level and adjust by tamping if

necessary. Remove excess mortar with a trowel and return it to the mortar board for reuse. If necessary, leave weep holes by omitting the mortar from every third joint. This will allow excess water to escape freely from the raised bed.

13 Raise the string lines and then lay both rows of the second course. Remember to stagger the brickwork joints in each row as this will give the brickwork strength.

14 The bricks of the top course are laid in header bond on edge across the double row of brickwork. Start the header course by laying three or four bricks at each end. Check for level and then set a string line at the front of the course only. Use a spirit level to level the back of the header bricks. Spread two lines of mortar as a base for the header bricks. Butter the side of each brick, position it to the string line and tap it into place. Keep the joints at about 8 mm.

15 Continue to lay the header course until approximately 1.5 m

remains. Measure the gap left to determine whether the remaining joints should be opened or closed so that you can finish the work using full bricks. This is easier than having to cut bricks.

ADDING THE CURVED SIDE
16 The bricks in the curved side are laid across the footing in header bond, to make the curve more gradual and to avoid excessive brick cutting. Measure, mark and cut the first brick of the base course. Spread a double line of mortar along the footing. Butter the side of each brick before positioning it. To keep the curve even, lay the face of the bricks flush with the front of the footing. Lay the entire base course, constantly checking for level with a spirit level as string lines cannot be used. In tight parts of the curve, cut away the back edge of the brick with a bolster to keep the joints at the front even and no more than 15 mm wide.

17 Lay the second course of curved brickwork in a similar way, staggering the joints.

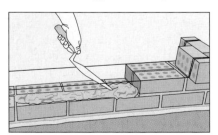

13 *Raise the string lines and lay both rows of the second course, staggering the brickwork joints.*

16 *Spread a double line of mortar on the footing and lay the first curved course across the footing.*

18 Measure, mark and cut the first two bricks of the header course to fit. Lay the cut bricks and then continue with full bricks. Use the spirit level to check for level and plumb. At the other end, where the curved side of the structure meets the straight side, measure, mark and cut the final two bricks. Butter the cut bricks, position them and tap them into place.

TO FINISH

19 Rake the joints with a joint raker once the mortar is sufficiently dry, and then clean down the brickwork, first by brushing the jointwork with a small brush and then by washing down the brick surface with clean water and a sponge. If the bricks are not washed down now, the mortar leaves stains that will be difficult to remove later.

20 Fill the base of the bed to the height of the drainage holes or slots with a free-draining gravel. Top this gravel with soil to the required height and plant out the garden bed as desired.

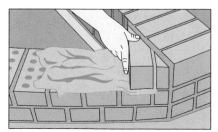

18 Begin laying the header course with the cut bricks and then continue with full bricks.

MIXING CONCRETE

Concrete can be ordered ready-mixed, or you can hand-mix it for small jobs. To mix concrete yourself, use a 4:2:1 ratio of four parts coarse aggregate (gravel), two parts fine aggregate (sand) and one part cement. Coarse aggregate comes in a variety of sizes up to 20 mm, but you will find 10 mm easiest to use.

HAND MIXING

Using a levelled-off bucket, mix appropriate ratios of fine and coarse aggregate and cement in a dry state, either in a wheelbarrow or on a large, flat board. Make a well in the centre and add water, mixing to an even consistency.

USING A CONCRETE MIXER

Place 20–25 litres of water in the mixer. Add four level bucketsful of coarse aggregate (gravel), and then two buckets of fine aggregate (sand) and, finally, one bucket of cement. Repeat the procedure if the capacity of the mixer allows. Mix to an even consistency.

READY-MIXED CONCRETE

Ready-mixed concrete is delivered in quantities that increase by 0.2 m³. The product description for edges and garden footings is Gen 3/ST4, which can withstand 20 Newtons/mm² and contains 10 mm coarse aggregate.

Concrete makes a sturdy raised garden bed. The concrete can be coloured or given a textured finish if desired so that it blends more easily into the landscape. This bed was given a coat of textured paint.

Concrete raised bed

Concrete is an ideal material for a raised bed but ensure you provide adequate drainage so that the soil inside does not become waterlogged. It is essential that the formwork is constructed accurately and is strong enough to contain the wet concrete.

CONSTRUCTING THE FORMWORK

1 Mark out the 1800 x 1200 mm sheet of plywood, dividing it lengthways into four strips 300 mm wide. Likewise, mark out the 1200 x 1200 mm sheet into four strips 300 mm wide. Cut the strips using a circular saw, with a straight edge as a guide, or a handsaw.

2 On two 1800 mm pieces, measure along 1484 mm and mark the length, and on two 1200 mm pieces measure and mark the length at 884 mm. Nail the two pairs together and cut the lengths square.

3 Construct the outside box using two 1800 mm and two 1200 mm lengths (see the diagram on page 30). Nail the butt joints together using 65 x 3 mm plywood nails, but nail only to the first head. This will allow you to remove the nails easily when dismantling the formwork. Use three equally spaced nails per joint.

4 The inside box cannot be nailed together like the outside one because once the concrete is poured it is impossible to remove the nails.

MATERIALS*

- 1800 x 1200 mm sheet of 18 mm plywood
- 1200 x 1200 mm sheet of 18 mm plywood
- Timber pegs
- Four 300 mm long 75 x 50 mm softwood cleats
- 1400 mm long piece of 50 x 25 mm timber for spreader
- Six 500 mm long pieces of 50 x 25 mm timber for buttresses
- Ten 140 mm long 50 x 25 mm timber spacer blocks
- 40 x 3 mm lost-head nails
- 65 x 3 mm lost-head plywood nails
- 18 mm flexible plastic conduit
- 6 m of three-bar steel reinforcement, tie wire and bar men
- Vegetable cooking oil or motor oil
- Cement
- Sand
- Coarse aggregate (gravel)

* To construct a garden bed 1800 x 1164 mm and 300 mm high.

Therefore, nail 300 mm long timber cleats flush to both ends of the long sides, using three 40 x 3 mm lost-head nails. Position the short ends of the

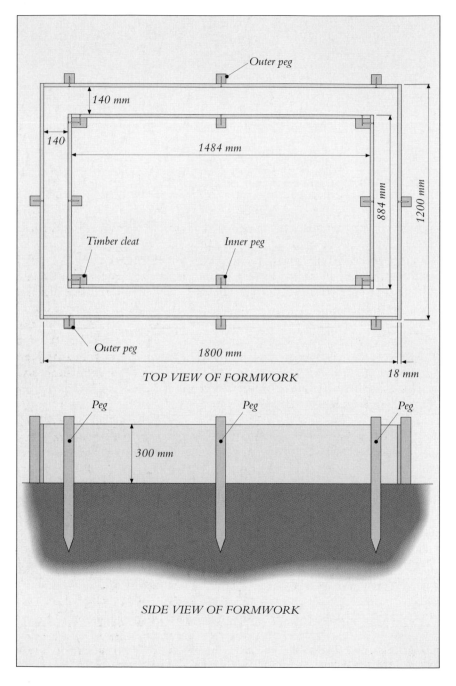

Outer peg

140 mm

140

1484 mm

884 mm

1200 mm

Timber cleat

Inner peg

Outer peg

1800 mm

18 mm

TOP VIEW OF FORMWORK

Peg

Peg

Peg

300 mm

SIDE VIEW OF FORMWORK

box and nail through the plywood into the timber cleat with two nails.

5 Prepare the 1836 x 1200 mm site, removing grass or unwanted vegetable matter. Roughly level the ground to make it easier to position the boxes.

6 Position the outside box on the ground and measure both diagonals to ensure it is square. Adjust and temporarily brace across the corners if necessary. Position three outer pegs equally spaced along each long side against the formwork, driving them in with a sledge or club hammer until they are firm. Add a peg in the middle of each short side. Use a spirit level to ensure the sides are level. If necessary, prop up the sides to the correct height before fixing them to the pegs with 40 x 3 mm lost-head nails. Nail only once near the top of the sides to make dismantling easier.

7 Position the inside box, ensuring there is an even 140 mm space between the inside and outside boxes. Position an inner peg against

TOOLS

- Basic tools (see page 13)
- Circular saw or handsaw
- Chisel
- Electric drill
- 18 mm hole saw or spade bit
- Steel mesh cutters or angle grinder
- Edging tool
- Paintbrush

each inner face of the inside box, in the centre of each side, and once again drive it into the ground until it is firm. Lay a spirit level or straight edge across both boxes and lift and adjust the inside box to exactly match the finished height of the outside box. Fix it by nailing through the top of the plywood into the pegs, using one 40 x 3 mm lost-head nail per peg.

FINISHING THE FORMWORK

8 As concrete is particularly heavy when wet, strengthen the box so that it doesn't lose shape or move sideways during the pour. Place the

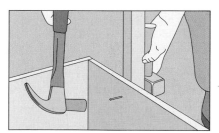

6 Ensure the sides are level before fixing them to each peg with one nail near the top of the side.

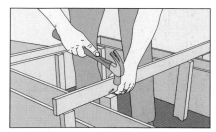

8 Place the spreader across the centre of the long sides, nailing it to the tops of the centre pegs.

spreader across the centre of the long sides. Check that the sides of the box are parallel and equally spaced before fixing the spreader to the tops of the centre pegs using 40 x 3 mm lost-head nails.

9 To prevent the formwork flexing sideways, hammer in extra pegs about 250 mm outside the box. Nail buttresses to the outer pegs at the level of the top of the sides and then angle them down and fix them to the extra pegs at ground level.

10 To provide drainage holes through the concrete, drill 18 mm holes through both boxes. Position the holes 50 mm above ground level and every 600 mm along the outside box (line up the holes in the inside box with these). Place 18 mm plastic conduit through the pairs of holes to provide a channel for the water (the ends will be trimmed off later).

11 Using steel mesh cutters or an angle grinder, cut two 1700 mm and two 1100 mm lengths of three-bar steel reinforcement. Position the

lengths between the sides about 50 mm above ground level on bar men and tie the corners together with tie wire.

12 Cut ten 140 mm long timber spacer blocks, and space them equally within the formwork to help keep the sides parallel. As the concrete is poured, gradually lift them higher until the concreting is completed and the spacer blocks are finally removed.

13 Use a paintbrush to coat the inside of the formwork with oil. This will make removal of the formwork easier and prevent the concrete surface honeycombing.

ADDING THE CONCRETE

14 Mix the concrete (see page 27) and pour it into the formwork. This can be a difficult job, so consider carefully whether to mix it yourself or have it delivered. Ensure there is access to the site, and construct a wheelbarrow ramp if necessary.

15 Once the concrete is in place, level the surface with a float. Tap the

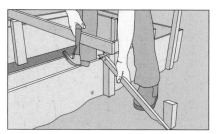

9 Fix buttress supports to the outer pegs, angle them down and fix them to the extra pegs at ground level.

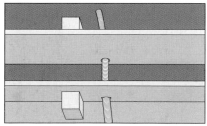

10 Drill holes through both boxes and place plastic conduit through the holes as a channel for the water.

formwork sides with a hammer to help settle the concrete, remove air pockets and prevent honeycombing on the surface. Run an edging tool along both sides of the top surface to push the aggregate down.

16 Allow the concrete to set for 1–2 hours. Once the top of the concrete feels firm when pressed, finish the top surface with an edger.

17 Remove the nails from the outside formwork only and begin to pull it away. If the concrete does not wobble or move, it is safe to continue. Weather conditions can affect the drying time of concrete, so if there is any movement wait for another hour.

18 Use a wooden float on the vertical face, working horizontally to prevent damage to the top edge. The wooden float will give the surfaces a textured look. Fill any holes in the surfaces with a mix of one part sand and one part cement. It is best to float from the corners to the centre to prevent damage to the edges.

TO FINISH

19 Allow the concrete to set fully. Split the cleats away with a hammer and chisel and pull away and lift out the inside formwork.

20 Cut off the drainage pipes so that they are flush with the surface of the concrete. Fill the base of the garden bed with a layer of broken bricks, tiles or gravel for drainage before adding soil and compost.

CONCRETE FOOTINGS

The size of the footing for a masonry raised bed is determined by what you will plant in the bed. Large trees will lift and crack small footings. To contain them, a footing 300 mm wide and deep, reinforced with a three-bar steel cage, is appropriate. For smaller trees, shrubs or palms, a footing 300 mm wide and 100 mm deep with a single layer of three-bar steel reinforcing or trench mesh is sufficient. For annuals and small plants, a brick footing below ground level is adequate.

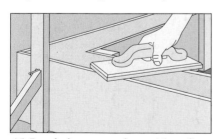

15 Level the top surface with a float wide enough to bear on both the inner and outer boxes.

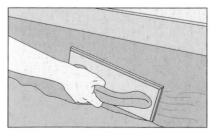

18 Use a wooden float on the vertical face, working horizontally to prevent damage to the top edge.

Building retaining walls

Retaining walls are built to retain, support or hold back an area of garden or soil – although they may also support a fence, wall or garden. They are often used to alter a sloping site, by providing a series of level terraces.

PLANNING

Retaining walls must be carefully planned if they are to be strong and durable. Walls more than about 1 m high can have extreme pressure exerted on them by expansive clay soils and trapped water. For this reason, it is better practice to design a series of smaller walls that make up a terrace, rather than constructing one large single wall, which may be unable to withstand the pressures exerted on it. In addition, it is worth checking with your local council's planning authority before beginning any major retaining wall, because you may need to submit plans with engineering specifications.

MATERIALS

Materials commonly used in retaining walls include timber, brick, masonry blocks and stone.
• Timbers that are suitable for retaining walls include hardwood and treated pine products such as logs, splits and slabs, as well as both old and new railway sleepers.
• All bricks, both dry pressed and extruded, are suitable for retaining walls, but you should have some bricklaying experience before you

begin to build a brick retaining wall.
• Concrete blocks are easier and faster to lay than bricks. They range from the traditional rectangular blocks to a variety of solid interlocking styles suitable for dry stacked walls.
• Stone retaining walls have been used for thousands of years. The stone can be sawn or cut to shape, or it can be used in its rough form. Stone can be dry stacked or finished with mortared joints.

TERRACING A SLOPE

Careful planning can save time and money if you are going to use retaining walls to terrace a slope. First draw a detailed plan or layout of the site. If you intend to use the area for entertaining, ensure that the terrace will be large enough to accommodate tables and chairs and allow free movement around them. Determine the location of steps, ramps and interconnecting paths, remembering that it is easier to negotiate a series of short steps than one steep climb.

Try to work around existing trees to avoid having to remove them or damage root systems, and check the

A series of retaining walls, each about a metre high, have been built here to terrace a steeply sloping site. The rendered masonry walls have been finished with stone coping blocks.

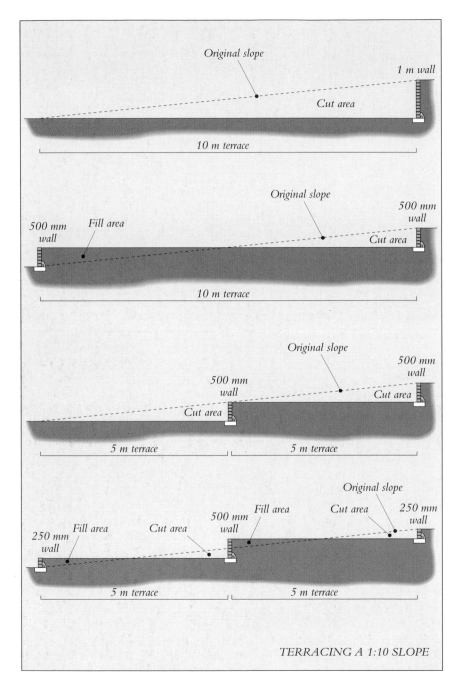

TERRACING A 1:10 SLOPE

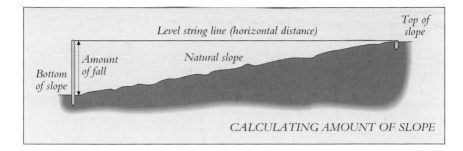

Level string line (horizontal distance)

Top of slope

Amount of fall

Natural slope

Bottom of slope

CALCULATING AMOUNT OF SLOPE

angle and position of the sun for any proposed gardens or shade areas.

Decide whether the walls will be straight or curved, and vertical or angled. Work out how any drainage problems can be overcome. If a wall will be so high that it may not be strong enough, check whether you could achieve suitable terraces using two smaller walls. Smaller walls require less engineering and take less time and expertise to build.

Once the terrace has been cut, the retaining wall should be constructed only on the cut-out section. Never build a wall on a filled area as this ground will continue to settle and move for some time.

Remember, too, the extra costs involved in excavation and removal of unwanted soil. If a landfill site is available close by, this may not be a problem. If not, it would be best to use a method that moves the soil from one area of the site to another.

DETERMINING THE SLOPE
When deciding on the size of the retaining walls you will have to know how much slope, or fall, is on the site.

1 Stretch a taut, level string line from the top of the slope to the bottom. Use a spirit level to make sure the string line is level (see the diagram above).

2 At the bottom of the slope measure the vertical distance from the string line to the ground to determine the fall.

3 Measure the horizontal distance of the slope along the level string line.

4 Use these two measurements to create a slope ratio. For example, a fall of 1 m over a horizontal distance of 10 m gives a ratio of 1:10. This means that for every 10 m the land falls 1 m.

CHOOSING THE TERRACING METHOD
The vertical fall will determine the total height of the retaining walls and the horizontal distance determines the amount of space available to divide into terraces. Four possible ways of terracing a 10 m site that has a fall of 1 m are shown in the diagram opposite.

EXCAVATION

Once the planning and preparation have been taken care of, excavation can begin. This is a difficult and time-consuming process and it is often advisable to employ machinery. Machines such as bobcats or backhoes can be hired with a driver for a reasonable cost, and they can complete in 1–2 hours what could take a week of manual labour.

Before work starts, mark out the location of the cuts on the ground, using lime or flour, and note the location of any underground cables, telephone lines or water pipes. If you are using machinery, be sure to tell the operator where these are and how deep the cuts are to be.

Most operators will remove unwanted earth, but check that this is included in the price quoted.

PROVIDING DRAINAGE

Whenever a natural slope undergoes a cut and fill process, there will be problems with drainage because the natural run-off or water course has been disrupted. It is essential that adequate drainage is provided behind a retaining wall, regardless of its size. If drainage is ignored, structural problems will occur later.

WEEP HOLES

To prevent water building up at the back of a solid retaining wall, incorporate weep holes into the base course of brick or block work. They allow water to seep down the slope. To create weep holes in brickwork, leave every third vertical joint free of mortar, and in block work leave every second vertical joint free. Alternatively, lay 15 mm plastic pipes, cut to the thickness of the wall, in each of the free vertical joints.

Walls of logs or stacked rock have natural seepage points and it is not necessary to incorporate weep holes.

AGRICULTURAL PIPE

Water can also be diverted through agricultural pipe and gravel channels located at the back of the retaining wall. The water is then channelled to escape points, usually at one or both ends of the wall. Agricultural pipe can be covered with fabric or fine mesh, to prevent soil penetrating and possibly clogging the pipe. Agricultural pipe is usually sold in 20 m lengths. Both 65 mm and 100 mm diameter pipes are available in either covered or plain form.

GRAVEL

Gravel is an excellent drainage material, filtering excess water while retaining soil. It should be placed behind the retaining wall before you backfill with soil. Gravel comes in a variety of sizes from 5 to 20 mm in diameter. The most suitable size for drainage purposes is 10 mm as it is easy to shovel yet substantial enough to do the job; 20 mm gravel will provide good drainage, but is much heavier to manipulate.

Rubble such as broken terracotta tiles, brick and stone can also be used for drainage.

GEOTEXTILE FABRIC

If uncovered agricultural pipe is used, it is best to wrap the pipe and gravel surrounding it completely with geotextile fabric to ensure soil does not clog the gravel and pipe (see the diagram on page 43). Geotextile fabric, sometimes called 'terrum', is a filter fabric that keeps out soil but allows water through. It is sold in 2 m and 4 m widths and is available from most builders' merchants.

Walls of logs or stacked rock often have countless seepage points, but this can also mean that soil is washed out. To prevent this, geotextile fabric can be positioned at the back of the wall before backfilling with soil.

DISH DRAINS

To carry away extra surface run-off, dish drains can be created at both the top and bottom of the wall. These are open drains made from paving bricks, terracotta or PVC pipe, ready-made channel or concrete. They catch and divert excess water.

BACKFILLING

Once the wall has had time to dry and settle, and drainage measures have been taken, the area behind the wall can be backfilled to the level required. Always backfill with light, sandy loam soils as clay-based soils will hold moisture and swell, placing extra pressure on the wall.

Where soil needs to be stabilised behind large, dry-stacked masonry walls, geogrid soil reinforcement mesh can be used for extra stability.

BASIC STEPS IN RETAINING WALL CONSTRUCTION

1 Make a simple sketch or drawing showing the shape plus the necessary dimensions of height, length and width, as well as the placement of any steps or ramps.

2 If necessary, obtain engineering specifications, plan drawings and council approval.

3 Set out the site to determine the location of the wall.

4 Cut out the site and relocate or remove the excavated soil, using machinery if necessary. Excavate any footings required.

5 If footings are required, position the steel reinforcement, pour the concrete and level it. Allow 2–3 days for the footings to dry.

6 Construct the wall to the desired height.

7 Position drainage material such as agricultural pipe, geotextile fabric and free-draining gravel behind the wall.

8 Backfill behind the wall with light, sandy soil.

9 In areas with heavy run-off, position surface drains at the top and/or bottom of the wall.

These concrete blocks were laid precisely to a string line before the cores were filled with concrete. The wall was capped with matching blocks to hide the cores and provide a neat finish.

Concrete block retaining wall

Concrete blocks are fast and easy to lay, and the hollow core ensures they are not too heavy to lift. Filled with concrete and laid on a reinforced footing, they make a strong retaining wall.

PLANNING

The height of a concrete block wall determines the size of the footing and the steel reinforcement. Check your local building authority regulations and engineering specifications for appropriate sizes. Usually, for a small wall, concrete footings are twice as wide as the wall and as deep as the wall is wide, so for a wall 200 mm wide, the footing will be 400 mm wide and 200 mm deep.

PREPARATION

1 Establish the position of your wall and drive in a long peg at either end. If possible, position the pegs beyond the ends of the wall.

2 Mark the finished height of the wall on one peg. Transfer this mark to the other peg using a water level (see page 9). Mark down the face of both pegs the finished height of each course of blockwork. Remember to allow 8–10 mm for a mortar joint between courses.

3 Set a taut string line between the pegs, at the finished height of the wall if possible. If the line has to be squared off an existing structure such as a wall, use the 3-4-5 method (see

---

MATERIALS

- Timber for formwork
- Timber pegs
- 65 x 3 mm lost-head nails
- Three-bar steel reinforcement mesh and tie wire
- Starter bars or 12 mm steel rod
- Sand, cement and 10 mm aggregate (gravel) for concrete
- Sand, cement, lime and plasticiser for mortar
- Concrete blocks 390 x 190 x 190 mm
- Concrete blocks 390 x 95 x 190 mm for base course
- Half blocks 190 x 190 x 190 mm
- Concrete coping blocks 390 x 190 x 40 mm
- Waterproofing agent or black plastic
- Agricultural pipe and gravel
- Geotextile fabric (optional)

---

the box on page 8) or a builders square. Use a spirit level to check that the line is level.

4 Cut the bank and excavate the trench for the footing to the required depth and width. As you dig the trench, check the depth against the set string line using a measuring tape. To ensure that the footing will be

TOOLS

- Basic tools (see page 13)
- Water level
- Builders' square
- Bucket
- Concrete mixer (if available)
- Mortar board
- Steel mesh cutters or angle grinder
- Brick saw or circular saw with a masonry blade
- Line pins and corner blocks for holding string line (optional)
- Bricklaying trowel
- Round iron jointer
- Brush
- Sponge and bucket

level, position formwork at the front edge, held by pegs every 1200 mm.

5 Position one layer of three-bar mesh in the trench. Prepare the starter bars (see the box on page 45). The first is placed 100 mm from the end of the wall and approximately 100 mm back from the front of the footing. Place the horizontal end of

the starter bar beneath the mesh and tie them together twice with tie wire. The remaining starter bars are spaced every 400 mm, which is one per concrete block allowing for the 10 mm joints. Tie them to the mesh in the same way. Check the spacing of the bars.

6 To keep the starter bars vertical, tie the top of each bar to a length of horizontally positioned rod. Suspend the mesh and starter bars so that they are centrally located within the footing. This can be done by placing lengths of timber across the trench, supporting them on props where necessary. The mesh and starter bars can then be hung from the timber.

CONCRETING

7 Calculate the quantity of concrete required by measuring the length, width and depth of the footing. Order a delivery of concrete or mix your own (see page 27).

8 Pour the concrete. Using a straight edge and working from the front formwork, level the concrete. Check

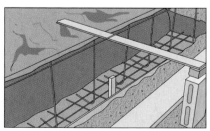

6 Tie the starter bars to a horizontal rod and suspend the mesh and starter bars centrally within the footing.

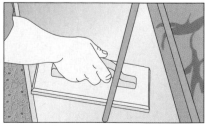

8 Pour the concrete and level it with a straight edge, before finishing the surface with a float.

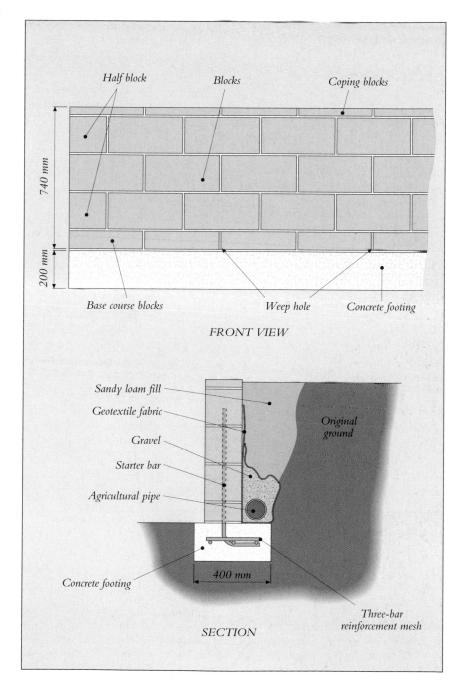

FRONT VIEW

SECTION

regularly with a spirit level as you work. Finish the concrete with a float and allow it to set for 2–3 days. Remove the horizontal rod.

LAYING THE BLOCKS

9 Lay out the base course of blocks dry on the footing and use a pencil to mark the positions of the end blocks on the concrete.

10 Prepare a mortar mix (see step 9 on page 25). Lay one block at each end of the wall and set a string line between them at the front top edge. If your wall has a corner, use the 3-4-5 method (see page 8) or a builders square to ensure the right angle is accurate.

11 Build the ends or corners of the wall to the required height, using half blocks to stagger the jointing. Butter (add mortar to) the end of each block and tap it into place, ensuring that it is level with the string line.

12 Spread two lines of mortar on the footing where the back and front of the blocks will go, each line about a metre in length. Lay the base course, by buttering the end of each block, positioning it over the vertical rod and tapping it level to the string line. Leave out the vertical mortar joint in every second block as a weep hole. Check the blocks are level and vertical with a spirit level.

13 Reset the string lines for each course. Spread 1–2 m of mortar along the front and back edges of the last course. Butter the ends of three or four blocks at a time before lifting and tapping them into position level with the string line.

14 When the jointing is sufficiently dry, run an iron jointer over all the joints. Brush and then sponge down the surface of the blocks until they are clean. Allow the wall to dry for at least a day.

15 Mix concrete for the core filling as described on page 27, but make the mix wetter than normal and use 10 mm coarse aggregate so that the mix will flow into the holes easily.

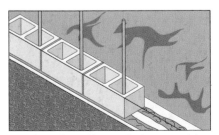

12 Spread two lines of mortar and lay the first course, positioning the blocks over the vertical rods.

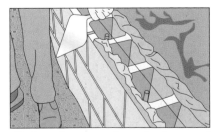

13 Spread mortar along the front and back edges of the blocks and lay the next course level with the string line.

16 Shovel or pour the concrete with a bucket into the cavities of each block. Tamp the concrete down with a piece of timber, finishing it level with the top of the blocks.

TO FINISH

17 To mitre the corner coping blocks, measure halfway along one and, with a marking pen, draw a line from there to the opposing corner. Repeat on a second block. Cut the mitres with a brick saw or a saw with a masonry blade.

18 Prepare a mortar mix and spread it on the wall to lay the first and last coping blocks. Position them so that the vertical joints along the wall will be staggered and use a spirit level to check for level. Set a string line to the front edge of these two end coping blocks.

19 Spread a mortar bed over the wall and make two or three furrows along it. Lay the coping blocks and check that the blocks stay aligned. Re-lay the last block if necessary to maintain the alignment of the joints.

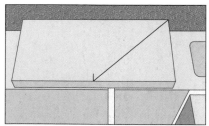

17 Measure half the block and, using a marking pen, draw a line from the halfway mark to the opposing corner.

STARTER BARS

Masonry walls are quite often reinforced with vertical steel rods known as starter bars. The vertical rods are tied to the mesh or cage in the footing and provide great strength to the wall.

Starter bars can be purchased ready-made with a 90 degree bend, or you can make your own from 12 mm steel bar. To do this, cut the bar into the desired lengths (900 mm for a 700 mm high wall), using steel mesh cutters or an angle grinder.

Measure the vertical length, in this case 700 mm, and mark the bar with a marking pen. Position the bar in a fixed length of pipe and flex or bend it to a 90 degree position at the 700 mm mark.

The starter bar will thus have a 200 mm base and, when set into the footing, will extend up into the top course.

20 Paint the back of the wall with a waterproofing agent or cover it with black plastic.

21 Position geotextile fabric behind and at the base of the wall, and lay agricultural pipe.

22 Cover the pipe with gravel for good drainage. If you have used uncovered agricultural pipe, wrap the pipe and gravel in geotextile fabric. Backfill the trench with sandy soil.

Dressed stone retaining wall

Dressed stone blocks were given a sawn edge on the front face to make it easier to align them and then laid with mortar to make this elegant wall. It is supported on a reinforced concrete footing.

PLANNING

As stone walls are very heavy, a strong footing is required. For this wall it is 400 x 300 mm and contains three steel rods at the top and bottom of the supporting stirrups.

Check with your local building authority to see if you should submit plans and footing specifications.

Always wear gloves when working with stone.

PREPARATION

1 Establish the position of the wall and drive in two long pegs, one at either end. If possible, position them beyond the ends of the wall and use a spirit level to check they are vertical. On one peg mark the finished height of the wall, and then the position of each course, allowing for 5–7 mm joints. Use a water level (see page 9) to transfer the marks to the other peg.

2 Excavate the footing to the required depth. Position timber formwork at the front edge of the footing, with pegs every 1200 mm, and ensure it is level.

3 Position steel reinforcement in the trench, elevating it on bar men or lifting it and tying it to timbers

MATERIALS

- Timber for formwork
- Timber pegs
- 65 x 3 mm lost-head nails
- Three-bar steel reinforcment mesh, tie wire and stirrups
- Bar men
- Sand, cement and 10 mm aggregate (gravel) for concrete
- Sand, cement, lime, yellow oxide and plasticiser for mortar
- Stone blocks 400 x 200 x 150 mm
- Stone coping blocks 400 x 75 x 200 mm
- Agricultural pipe
- Gravel for drainage
- Geotextile fabric (optional)

placed across the trench so it will be completely surrounded by concrete.

4 Calculate the quantity of concrete for the footing by measuring the length, width and depth. Order it or mix your own (see page 27).

5 Pour the concrete and use a spirit level and straight edge to level it (use the front formwork as a guide). Finish it with a wooden float. Let the concrete set for 2–3 days.

Sandstone, a soft sedimentary rock that is easy to cut and shape, was used for this retaining wall, but any dressed stone blocks can be laid in the same way. Coping blocks were added for a neat finish.

6 Sort the blocks into laying order, matching colours or patterns as desired. Cut and face them as necessary (see pages 50 and 51). The end of any return blocks will be exposed and should be finished in the same way as the front face.

7 Cut the end blocks to length to maintain the staggered joints (see the diagram on page 48). For a straight wall cut one 200 mm block. For a corner, cut two blocks 350 mm long.

LAYING THE BLOCKS
8 Prepare a mortar mix of five parts sand, one part cement and half a part lime or fireclay (5:1:½). A plasticiser

can be added to make the mix more workable. If desired, add a cup of coloured oxide for each shovel of cement. Mix the dry materials together thoroughly, and then add enough water to make a pliable but stiff mix (sandstone is very heavy and

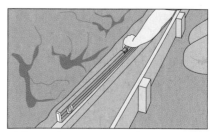

5 Pour the concrete and use a spirit level and straight edge to level it (the front formwork will act as a guide).

47

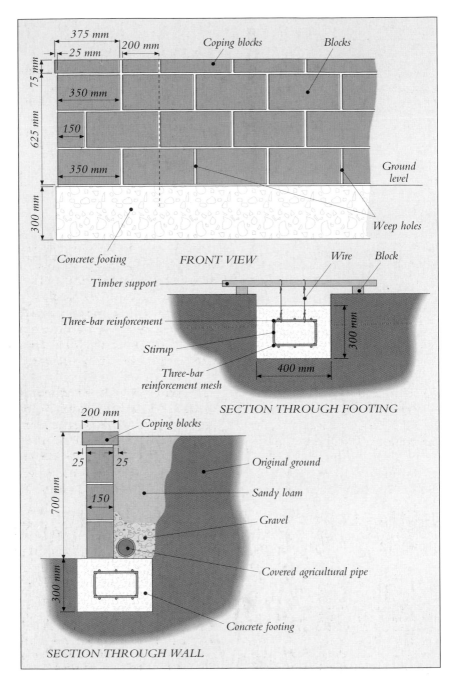

375 mm
25 mm
200 mm
Coping blocks
Blocks
75 mm
350 mm
625 mm
150
350 mm
Ground level
300 mm
Concrete footing
Weep holes

FRONT VIEW

Timber support
Wire
Block
Three-bar reinforcement
Stirrup
300 mm
Three-bar reinforcement mesh
400 mm

SECTION THROUGH FOOTING

200 mm
Coping blocks
25
25
Original ground
700 mm
150
Sandy loam
Gravel
Covered agricultural pipe
300 mm
Concrete footing

SECTION THROUGH WALL

TOOLS

- Basic tools (see page 13)
- Water level
- Builders' square
- Concrete mixer (if available)
- Mortar board
- Steel mesh cutters or angle grinder
- Brick saw or circular saw with masonry blade
- Masonry pencil
- Line pins and corner blocks for holding string lines (optional)
- Bricklaying trowel
- Round iron jointer
- Brush, sponge and bucket
- Gloves, safety goggles and respirator

will compress the mortar more than bricks do). Mortar is useful for only one and a half hours, so don't mix too much at a time. If you are using a cement mixer, double the mix to 10:2:1 and use one-third of a cup of plasticiser for two shovels of cement.

9 Transfer the mortar to a mortar board. To keep it soft and pliable it will need to be worked back and forth across the board with a trowel.

10 Establish the position of the first and last blocks of the base course. If there is to be a corner, the first block at that end is 350 mm long. Spread a bed of mortar for each block, position it and ensure it is level. Lay the corner and end stones of the return wall, using a builders square for an accurate right angle.

11 Stretch a taut string line along the front of the blocks. Lay the base course to the set string line. Spread a double line of mortar for the blocks to bed into and use the handle of a club hammer to tap them into place. Check for level. If weep holes are needed, omit mortar from every second vertical joint in this course.

12 Position and lay the first and last blocks of the second course. Repeat the laying procedure as for the first course, ensuring that the vertical joints are staggered (use the 200 mm block to begin if there is no corner). Continue for the third course (if

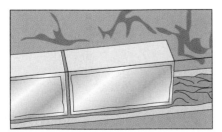

11 Lay the base course to the set string line, spreading a double line of mortar in which to bed the stones.

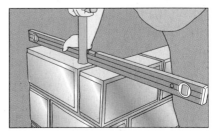

12 Continue laying for the third course, using a spirit level and tapping the block into position.

CUTTING STONE

Dressed stone is usually purchased from a quarry, but softer stones can be cut at home.

The easiest way is with a wet diamond-bladed brick saw, which can be hired. (Dry-cutting using a circular saw with a masonry blade creates a lot of dust.) A club hammer and bolster work on thinner cuts. For thick pieces of stone, cut part of the way through the stone on all four sides with a blade and then complete the cut by driving wedges or the bolster into the cut, forcing the stone to split.

Before you begin, prepare a good solid bench at a height that will allow you to stand upright. Place a piece of stone beneath the stone that is being cut. This eliminates any bounce. The surface of these supporting blocks should be kept clear of grit and dust to ensure an even cutting surface. Always wear goggles and a respirator when cutting stone.

---

there is a corner, begin with a 350 mm block). Finish the joints with a round iron jointer, brush down the stone and sponge it clean.

13 Cut the coping blocks. These are usually smaller in height but wider than the wall blocks to allow a small overhang each side. Position them dry on the wall, maintaining the staggered joints.
• For straight walls cut the end block to 225 mm (for a 25 mm overhang).

14 Lay the coping blocks, using a builders' square to ensure any corners form a right angle.

• For a corner, cut the block to 375 mm. To prepare a mitre, measure halfway along and, with a masonry pencil, draw a line from the mark to the opposing corner. Repeat the mitre on a second block. Cut the mitres with a brick saw or a saw with a masonry blade. Cut the second coping block to 200 mm. Once the mitred corner and the second block are in place, stagger the joints to match the rest of the wall.

14 Lay the coping blocks following the same procedure as for the wall blocks, checking for square at the corners with a builders square.

15 Allow the mortar to dry. Brush and sponge the stone clean. Position agricultural pipe and gravel behind the wall, wrapping them with geo-textile fabric if necessary. Backfill with sandy soil.

DRESSING STONE

Dressing stone is a time-consuming process, so don't try to hurry. It takes 5–10 minutes to dress and face each block.

Select the best-looking and more convex surface of each block to face. Using a masonry pencil and a square, scribe a straight line around the four sides, 10–15 mm back from the surface to be edged or faced. This is the cutting line.

A SAWN EDGE AND ROCK FACE

To dress the edges of the front face, use a circular saw with a masonry blade, a club hammer and a bolster. Two people are needed, one person cutting as the other holds the straight edge. Both must wear protective clothing, safety goggles and a respirator.

1 Set a timber straight edge in position as a guide. Set the depth of cut on the saw at 15 mm. (Check and reset it every four or five blocks as the blade will wear down as it cuts.) With your helper holding the straight edge in position, make a 15 mm deep cut around the four sides of the block. The cuts must align at each corner of the block.

2 Place a bolster in the cut and strike it firmly with a club hammer. Work around the cut until the edges have been struck away, leaving the sawn edge exposed and the front of the block rock faced.

A ROCK FACE FINISH

If the stone is not to have a sawn edge, use the scribed line as a guide for your bolster.

Make the initial blows with the hammer lighter to create a cutting groove and then increase the blows until the stone comes away in a straight line. Work around the line until the edges of the block have been struck away, leaving the front surface rock faced.

1 With your helper holding the straight edge in position, make a 15 mm deep cut around the face.

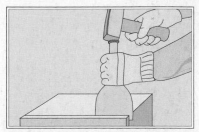

2 Place a bolster in the cut and strike the bolster firmly with a club hammer.

Naturally weathered rock was purchased from a garden supplier and fitted together neatly to produce this sturdy dry-stone wall, but a similar result could have been obtained using any naturally shaped or rough-hewn stone.

Dry-stone retaining wall

Dry-stone walls are attractive and durable, and they can be very strong if time is taken to fit the stones together tightly. For extra strength the stones in this wall are bedded in concrete.

PLANNING

Small dry-stone walls can be constructed without a concrete footing, but in that case the base stones should be half-buried in the ground to prevent movement. In this project, a footing approximately 100 mm deep was excavated to contain a concrete bedding for the base stones.

The wall stones can be dry-stacked or a shallow bed of concrete can be placed beneath each individual stone for greater stability. The concrete is not visible from the front and so does not affect the appearance of the wall. If you are bedding the stones in concrete, it is best to have two people working on the project, one person positioning the stones as the other person mixes the concrete and backfills the wall as

TOOLS

- Basic tools (see page 13)
- Long pegs (or 2 m lengths of 12 mm steel rod)
- Water level
- Concrete mixer (if available)
- Brush
- Sponge
- Bucket
- Gloves

it increases in height. Always wear gloves when working with stone.

Remember to check with your local building authority; and consult an engineer to ensure that the proposed wall is not too high to withstand the pressures that will be exerted on it.

SELECTING STONES

To create the best-looking and most stable dry-stone wall, take time over your selection of the stones. Choose stones that are square and chunky in shape, as these fit together more easily than round or oval shapes. The stones should fit together with a minimum of gaps so that soil will be retained efficiently and not gradually dribble through the joints.

MATERIALS

- Selected stone
- Cement
- Sand
- 10 mm coarse aggregate (gravel)
- Agricultural pipe
- Gravel for drainage
- Geotextile fabric (optional)

When choosing the stones for your wall, select three main sizes:

• Base stones for the foundation. These should be large and heavy (about 300–350 mm long) as they support the rest of the wall. Calculate the length of the wall in metres and multiply it by three to give the number of base stones needed. For example, 15 m x 3 = 45 base stones.

• Wall stones for the bulk of construction. These should be medium in size (about 250–300 mm long), with the larger ones laid lower in the wall than the small ones. To calculate the number of wall stones needed, multiply the length of the wall (15 m) by the height (0.8 m) and then multiply that by 10 (roughly the number of medium stones in 1 m^2): 15 x 0.8 = 12 m^2 and 12 x 10 = 120 wall stones.

• Head stones or copestones. These are the smaller, flatter stones (about 200 mm long) that are placed along the top of the wall to give it a level, neat finish. Head stones are usually seated in a bed of mortar or concrete to hold them firmly in place as they can be easily removed or knocked off the wall. To calculate the number of head stones required, multiply the length of the wall in metres by 5. For example, 15 m x 5 = 75 head stones.

PREPARATION

1 Establish the line of the wall and drive in a long peg or length of steel rod at either end. Position a string line between the two pegs, if possible at the finished height. Use a water level if required to ensure it is level (see the box on page 9).

2 Excavate or cut the bank along the desired line and create a 100 mm deep footing trench.

3 Examine the stones and separate them into the three groups. Grouping stones that seem to work together also saves a lot of time later. Remember that building a dry stone wall is like constructing a jigsaw: select and fit one piece at a time. Don't rush this sorting.

4 Position the large base stones in laying order approximately 500 mm in front of the footing trench. Spread the medium wall stones around just beyond the base stones. Position the small head stones on top of the bank if possible. This makes them easy to get to when you are laying the final course of stone.

5 Position the pegs at either end of the wall, at the front face of the wall,

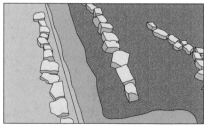

4 Position the base stones in front of the trench, the wall stones behind and the head stones on top of the bank.

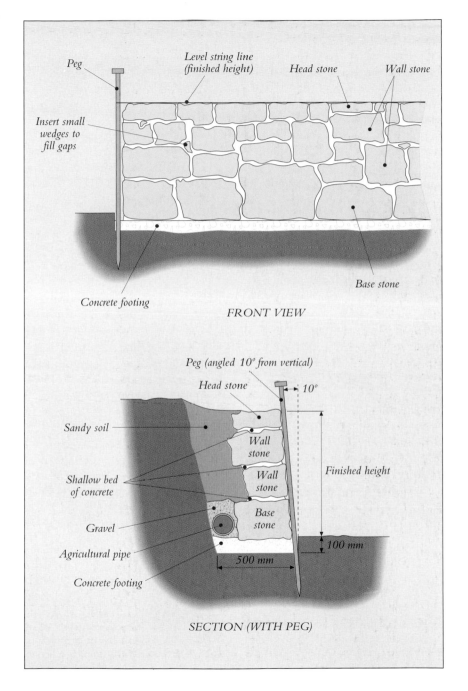

Peg

Level string line
(finished height)

Head stone

Wall stone

Insert small
wedges to
fill gaps

Concrete footing

Base stone

FRONT VIEW

Peg (angled 10° from vertical)

Head stone

10°

Sandy soil

Wall
stone

Finished height

Wall
stone

Shallow bed
of concrete

Base
stone

Gravel

100 mm

Agricultural pipe

500 mm

Concrete footing

SECTION (WITH PEG)

and make sure that they are approximately 400–500 mm away from the cut bank. Angle the pins backwards at about 10 degrees by measuring in from the vertical 100 mm for each 1 m of vertical height. The slant will give the wall greater strength and stability (see the diagram on page 55). Stretch at least two taut string lines between the pins, so that they provide a guide to the correct angle when you are laying the stone.

CONSTRUCTING THE WALL

6 Make a 4:2:1 mix of concrete (see page 27). Starting at one end of the wall, spread a bed of concrete – about 1 m at a time – and position the base stones in it, ensuring that the face of the stones matches the angle of the string lines. Proceed slowly and carefully, making sure that the stones butt closely together. Use stones of different sizes so that a mosaic effect is created, but remember that a square surface on the top edge will make laying the second course easier. Continue laying the base stones until the base course has been completed.

> ### HINT
>
> If a dry-stone wall is to be met by a grassed area at either the base, the top or both, you will find that mowing is easier if you make a 100 mm wide concrete mower strip at the junction of grass and retaining wall.

7 Lay agricultural pipe behind the base course and cover it with crushed stone or gravel to the top of the base course. Wrap the pipe and gravel in geotextile fabric if desired.

8 Adjust the two string lines upwards for the next course and construct it using the wall stones. Work in one direction, taking time to carefully select each stone. If a stone does not fit well, discard it and try another. Stagger the joints for strength. If desired, bed each wall stone in concrete, making sure the concrete is not visible from the front. To prevent backfill material being washed out through the joints, cover the back of the joints with some

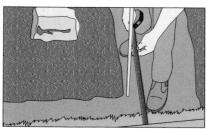

5 Position the pegs at either end of the wall, approximately 400–500 mm from the cut bank.

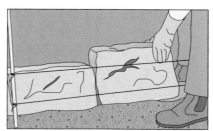

6 Butt the stones closely together in the concrete bed with the faces matching the angle of the string lines.

concrete as each piece is butted and bedded, or position geotextile fabric behind the wall. Backfill with gravel as you work.

9 Use small pieces or wedges of stone to fill any holes and help balance the stones. Tap them into place with a club hammer. Stone can be split with a club hammer and bolster to create smaller pieces of the required shape or size.

10 Repeat steps 8 and 9 to lay as many courses of wall stones as necessary for the final height.

FINISHING THE WALL

11 Before laying the smaller head stones, set a string line at the finished height. Check that it is level with a spirit level or water level.

12 To ensure the stability of these smaller pieces of stone, seat them in a shallow bed of concrete. Work from one end of the wall to the other, making sure that the selected pieces finish as close as possible to the final string line.

13 Check the wall and insert small wedges to fill any overly large crevices or to securely balance stones.

14 Wash down the face of the stone to remove any concrete stains. Backfill the wall to the finished height, using sandy, loam soil.

CURVED DRY-STONE WALLS

Dry-stone walling is the most suitable construction method for curved stone walls. They are easy to build, but you won't be able to use string lines to align the stones.

Mark the line of the wall on the ground with a rope or garden hose, or sprinkle a line of flour or lime on the ground.

To create the angled vertical surface, hold a spirit level vertical and measure in from it the required distance to position each stone. Calculate this for each course by measuring in from an end peg at the appropriate height. This is slower than laying to string lines, but a quality finish is possible with patience.

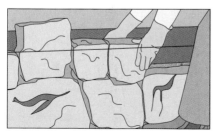

8 Construct the next course, carefully fitting each stone together and staggering the joints.

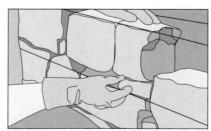

9 Use small pieces or wedges of stone to fill any holes between the larger stones and help balance them.

Timber slab retaining wall

This retaining wall consists of horizontal timbers resting on a bed of gravel to preserve them from decay. The timbers are held in place by posts against the outer face. Old railway sleepers were an ideal material.

PREPARATION

1 Establish the position of the wall and prepare the site by cutting away the bank. Position a long peg at each end of the future wall, preferably beyond the ends and aligned with the front of the wall. When driving in the pegs, angle them back at around 10 degrees by measuring in from the vertical 100 mm for every 1 m of vertical height.

2 Mark the finished height of the wall on one peg. Transfer this mark to the other peg using a string line and spirit level or a water level. Stretch a taut string line between the pegs at the finished height. Check that the line is level using a spirit

TOOLS

- Basic tools (see page 13)
- Water level (optional)
- Circular saw
- Power drill and drill bits
- Gloves

level. Measure down from the string line the height of the wall (allow for complete timbers so that you don't have to cut them), plus 50 mm for a bed of gravel.

3 Ensure the area for the gravel bed is roughly level and approximately 250–300 mm wide.

POSITIONING THE POSTS

4 Calculate the position of the posts on the outside of the wall. They should be centred every 2000–2400 mm, or so that the joints between the horizontal timbers are behind them. Wear gloves to protect your hands from splinters.

5 Dig holes approximately 400 mm in diameter and 500 mm deep for the posts. Place 100 mm of gravel in the base of each hole and tamp it down.

MATERIALS

- Long timber pegs or rods of steel bar
- Railway sleepers, or other logs or timber slabs (see page 62)
- Cement, sand and 10 mm aggregate (gravel)
- 75 x 3.5 mm galvanised lost-head nails
- Coach screws (optional)
- Geotextile fabric
- Agricultural pipe

Old railway sleepers, cut from hardwood and weathered over many years, make an ideal material for retaining walls, although they are difficult to cut and are heavy to lift. If they are laid on edge, however, only half as many are needed.

6 Measure from the string line down to the top of the gravel in the holes to obtain the length for the posts. Using a circular saw, cut the posts to length. If you are using sleepers, lay each at right angles across two other sleepers so you can roll it as you cut.

7 Position a second string line between the two pegs, just above the ground. Locate each post in its hole and angle it back to align with the two string lines. Alternatively, set the angle for the post by holding a spirit level vertical and measuring back the

6 To cut a sleeper, lay it at right angles across two others and roll it over as you cut.

7 Set the angle for the post using a vertical spirit level and a tape, or align it with the two string lines.

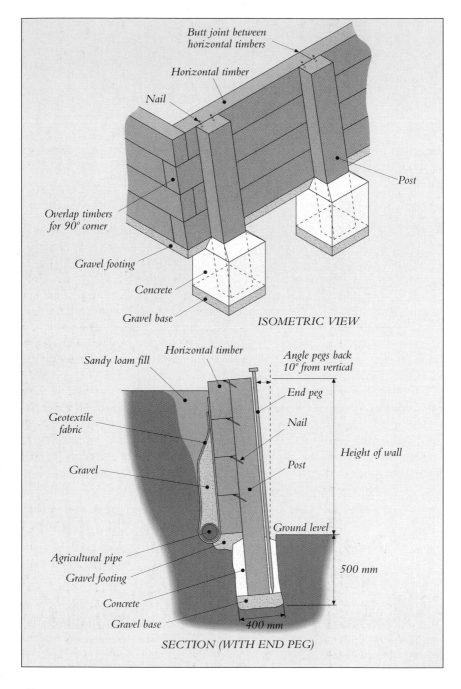

Butt joint between
horizontal timbers

Horizontal timber

Nail

Post

Overlap timbers
for 90° corner

Gravel footing

Concrete

Gravel base

ISOMETRIC VIEW

Sandy loam fill

Horizontal timber

Angle pegs back
10° from vertical

End peg

Nail

Geotextile
fabric

Gravel

Height of wall

Post

Agricultural pipe

Ground level

Gravel footing

Concrete

500 mm

Gravel base

400 mm

SECTION (WITH END PEG)

required distance. Make sure that the top of the post is exactly level with the top string line so that you won't have to cut it off later.

8 Mix concrete (see page 27). Check each post is at the correct angle with a spirit level and tape, and then fill the hole around it with concrete to 50 mm below the bottom string line. Angle the top of the concrete away from the post. Allow it to set.

LAYING THE SLABS

9 Fill the footing with gravel up to the bottom string line.

10 Set a string line and lay the base course of timbers on edge behind the posts, checking the timbers for level with a spirit level as they are positioned. Nail each timber in place using 75 x 3.5 mm galvanised lost-head nails and nailing at an angle through the top of the timber and into the post. If you are using old railway sleepers, first drill holes with a 4 mm bit as you will have difficulty nailing into the old hardwood. At right-angled corners use butt joints,

reversing the timbers for each layer so that they overlap and trimming the ends to fit together neatly.

11 Adjust the string lines up 240 mm, or the width of the timber, for each course and lay the remaining courses. Nail each course to the posts; the wall can be made more stable by attaching the top course with coach screws.

TO FINISH

12 Cover the back of the sleeper wall with geotextile fabric, making sure that there is sufficient fabric in the bottom of the footing to fully contain the agricultural pipe and gravel. The fabric will keep the backfill from direct contact with the timber and prevent premature decay, while allowing water to drain away.

13 Position the agricultural pipe behind the base course and inside the geotextile fabric. Cover it completely with gravel, filling as far up the wall as possible. Wrap the fabric around the gravel and pipe to form a bag. Backfill with sandy soil.

10 Nail each timber in place, nailing at an angle through the top of the timber and into the post.

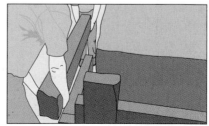

11 Adjust the string lines up the width of your timber and then lay the remaining courses.

TIMBER RETAINING WALLS

The construction of timber retaining walls is usually straightforward and is easily managed by the home builder. All that is required is cutting, drilling and fixing with nails or screws.

SELECTING TIMBER

Timbers used for retaining walls must be extremely durable and strong. Most common are preservative-treated softwoods such as pine. The softwoods should have a hazard rating of at least medium (see Selecting timber on pages 18–19).

Old railway sleepers are popular, though they are not as durable. They can be purchased from specialist suppliers, and from some garden supply centres and mail-order companies.

TYPES OF WALLS

The strongest designs are the straight slab wall, the vertical timber wall and the cribwork design.

• To create a slab wall, sleepers or treated pine slabs or logs are laid horizontally on top of each other. They can be fixed by drilling vertical holes and driving long spikes of steel rod through the structure. They can also be held in place by positioning evenly spaced vertical posts either at the front or the rear of the wall. The base slab should be set completely in the ground on a bed of drainage material such as gravel to slow the decaying process.

• To construct a vertical retaining wall, stand sleepers, or pine slabs or logs vertically side by side. This is the only way a curved retaining wall can be created out of timber. The timber sits in a trench, on a base of gravel for drainage. This reduces the risk of early decay from excess moisture. To provide strength to the wall, the vertical timbers are set into the ground to a depth of one-third or a half of their length, depending on what they are retaining. They are then stabilised by concrete which is poured around the base. The vertical timbers can all finish at the one level or the height can be varied to provide a castellated finish. If the top is level, a metal strip can be fixed along the top to hold the timbers together.

• Sleepers and treated pine slabs are great for building cribwork walls, which can reach enormous heights while maintaining their strength. Cribwork walls consist of alternate layers of notched timber set at right angles to each other. The first layer is laid parallel to the bank, and the second layer runs into the bank. This ties the wall into the bank, creating a particularly strong bond. The alternating timbers create a chequerboard with holes that can be planted with trailing plants.

Tools for building edges and walls

Some of the most useful tools for building edges and retaining walls are shown below. Build up your tool kit gradually – most of the tools can be purchased from your local hardware store.

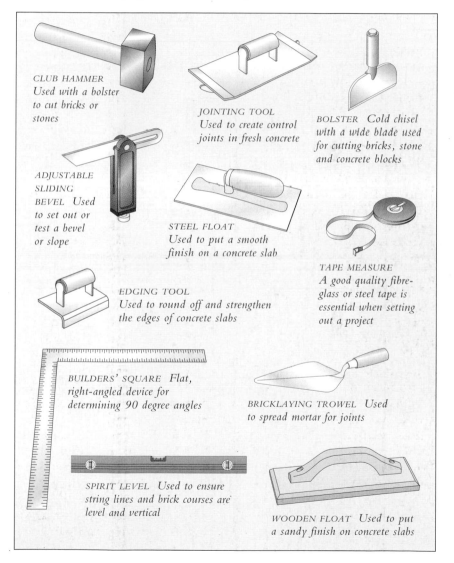

CLUB HAMMER Used with a bolster to cut bricks or stones

JOINTING TOOL Used to create control joints in fresh concrete

BOLSTER Cold chisel with a wide blade used for cutting bricks, stone and concrete blocks

ADJUSTABLE SLIDING BEVEL Used to set out or test a bevel or slope

STEEL FLOAT Used to put a smooth finish on a concrete slab

TAPE MEASURE A good quality fibre-glass or steel tape is essential when setting out a project

EDGING TOOL Used to round off and strengthen the edges of concrete slabs

BUILDERS' SQUARE Flat, right-angled device for determining 90 degree angles

BRICKLAYING TROWEL Used to spread mortar for joints

SPIRIT LEVEL Used to ensure string lines and brick courses are level and vertical

WOODEN FLOAT Used to put a sandy finish on concrete slabs

Index